Jörg Ziesak

The Dark Side of Personalization

Online Privacy Concerns influence Customer Behavior

Anchor Compact

Ziesak, Jörg: «Titel». The Dark Side of Personalization: Online Privacy Concerns influence Customer Behavior, Hamburg, Anchor Academic Publishing 2013
Original title of the thesis: The Dark Side of Personalization: How Personal Data Collection and Data Use influence Privacy Concerns, Personalization and Willingness to Transact

Buch-ISBN: 978-3-95489-061-3
PDF-eBook-ISBN: 978-3-95489-561-8
Druck/Herstellung: Anchor Academic Publishing, Hamburg, 2013
Additionally: «Hochschule», «Hochschulort», «Land», «Art»«Abgabe»

Bibliografische Information der Deutschen Nationalbibliothek:
Die Deutsche Nationalbibliothek verzeichnet diese Publikation in der Deutschen Nationalbibliografie; detaillierte bibliografische Daten sind im Internet über http://dnb.d-nb.de abrufbar

Bibliographical Information of the German National Library:
The German National Library lists this publication in the German National Bibliography. Detailed bibliographic data can be found at: http://dnb.d-nb.de

Purpose – This study establishes a link between different types of data collection, data usage and concerns for information privacy. It also analyses the impact of privacy concerns on value, risk and usability perception of personalization and the users' willingness to transact with the website.

Design / methodology / approach – This study develops a conceptual framework and tests it by collecting responses to a questionnaire from an online-crowdsourcing sample of Amazon Mechanical Turk.

Findings – The study reveals that both - open data collection as well as an unauthorized secondary use - increase concerns about information privacy. In the following, these concerns influence value and risks people perceive when confronted with personalization and also influence their perception of usability of the applied personalization method. Finally, the users' willingness to transact depends on a risk-value analysis when personalization is deployed.

Practical implications – The results of this study stress the importance of concerns reducing techniques marketers. The findings show that data collection and data use influence concerns for information privacy and its consequences. Reducing these concerns can be a meaningful way to improve value, risks and usability of personalization and, ultimately, customers' willingness to transact.

Research limitations / implications – The study focuses on a crowdsourcing sample from the United States. Future research may investigate the (international) generalizability of the findings. Moreover, future research could address, whether the findings differ when actual behavior is measured, instead of willingness to transact.

Originality / value – This is the first study to empirically examine the effects of different data collection and data use types on concerns for information privacy, perceptions of risk, value and usefulness of online personalization, and users' willingness to transact.

Paper type – Research paper.

Keywords – Personalization, privacy concerns, online data collection, unauthorized secondary use, willingness to share information

“The right of the people to be secure in their persons, houses, papers, and effects, against unreasonable searches and seizures, shall not be violated, and no Warrants shall issue, but upon probable cause, supported by Oath or affirmation, and particularly describing the place to be searched, and the persons or things to be seized”

Amendment IV, U.S. Bill of Rights (1791)

TABLE OF CONTENTS

List of Figures

List of Abbreviations

CFIP	Concerns for Information Privacy
ed.	Editor or Editors
et al.	et alii / et aliae / et alia
e.g.	Example given
U.S.	United States

1 Introduction

“Online Privacy Fears Stoked By Google, Twitter, Facebook Data Collection Arms Race” (Menn, 2012), “Your E-Book Is Reading You” (Alter, 2012), ""Instant personalization" brings more privacy issues to Facebook” (Keane, 2010). These are only a few recent examples of media headlines dealing with the issue of online privacy and personalization. Scholars and managers have repeatedly stated the benefits of personalization, which is targeting products and services to individual customers and constitutes a key element of an interactive marketing strategy (Montgomery & Smith, 2009). To be able to accurately estimate the needs and wants of customers, it is necessary to gather a significant amount of information. Privacy concerns may arise when personal information about customers are gathered. If this arises, personalization can backfire by making clients reluctant to use the service or - even worse - developing a negative attitude towards the company. A recent survey by Opera Software (2011) found, that Americans fear online privacy violations more than job losses or declaring personal bankruptcy. This had induced politicians to introduce regulations and laws that address online privacy that safeguard consumers against online monitoring and intrusion into confidential user information (Los Angeles Times, 2011). However, privacy online remains a complicated issue for both, managers and politicians, because new personalization technology emerges at a much faster pace than political regulations and guidelines.

Online users can only perceive privacy, if they are able to control their personal data. Prior literature has identified two prerequisites to determine the users’ control of information privacy: awareness of information collection and information usage (Sheehan & Hoy, 1999). Over the last two decades, the effects of privacy concerns has been investigated comprehensively (Yuan, 2011). Although insights in the social-psychology perspective of customer's information privacy concerns may be interesting for managers, most of the previous research focuses on general privacy concerns instead on information privacy (Laudon & Traver, 2008). Even less literature sheds light on the topic of information privacy in the context of personalization. A deeper understanding of the dimensions of control and their consequences is essential to fully understand the process online personalization. Especially if markets intend to deliver the best online personalization experience to their customers, these settings are of vital interest. Therefore, the goal of this study is to provide answers to the following research questions:

- What are the effects of different data collection methods (overt/covert) regarding private customer data on privacy concerns?
- How do different purposes of data usage (primary/ unauthorized secondary) influence concerns for information privacy and is this relationship influenced by trust that users have in the online merchant?
- Do users perform a risk-value analysis when personalization is applied by the online merchant?
- Do increased privacy concerns impact the evaluation of personalization and as a consequence users' willingness to transact?

These insights will provide marketers and advertising strategists with practical advice in order to implement an optimal personalization application for customers. Aiming to find answers to the research questions above, the paper will be structured as follows: First, the theoretical basis will be provided by a review on the existing literature and a conceptual model will be developed. As a conclusion of the literature review, hypotheses will be presented that create a basis for the experimental setting. Second, the conducted experiment, in which the model and the hypotheses were tested, will be described. Third, the results will be discussed and interpreted in detail. Finally, the last section will present theoretical and managerial implications, insights into limitations of the current study and suggestions for future research.

2 Literature Background

2.1 Personalization vs. Customization

Personalization occurs when a company tailors their product or service offerings to the individual tastes of their customers based on personal and preference information (Chellappa & Sin, 2005). To understand the principle of 'personalization', it has to be clearly distinguished from 'customization', which is defined as the users' ability to adapt certain criteria of the product offering, in order to better fit their individual needs (Laudon & Traver, 2008). While in customization the wish to adapt is initiated from the customer side, in personalization the marketer adapts the product or service to the customer by anticipating the customer's needs and wants (Chaffey, 2007; Montgomery & Smith, 2009). As such, researchers refer to customization as pull marketing and personalization as push marketing (Milne & Rohm, 2000). Hence, with respect to customization, users provide personal data voluntarily, while personalization requires firms to either ask for information or monitor and analyze customers' behavior, in order to adapt the product to individual needs.

2.2 Personalization in an Online Marketing Environment

Before personalization can take place, databases of collected personal consumer information have to be created. Data collection from online users is one of the fastest growing businesses on the online business (Angwin, 2010; Sipior, Ward, & Mendoza, 2011). Companies are able to collect an enormous amount of customer information, which can be used to deliver online experiences tailored specifically around the needs of each individual user (Ashworth & Free, 2006; Culnan, 1993; Pitta, Franzak, & Laric, 2003). This information can be divided into two groups: personally identifiable information and anonymous information. The former refers to data that enables identification, contact and discovery of an individual, while the latter refers to data that describes the individual but cannot be used to identify a specific person. Further, three subcategories of information types exist - contact information (name, address, phone, e-mail address), profile information (age, ethnicity, gender), and behavioral information (browsing and purchase history) on a single website or across multiple websites (Chaffey, 2007; Chellappa & Sin, 2005; Federal Trade Commission, 2000). The Internet enables firms to gather user data via multiple methods, which can be broadly classified as overt and covert information gathering techniques. Overt collections occur if firms ask users to answer direct questions. In this approach, users are aware of the fact that their data is gathered and used by the online company (Montgomery & Smith, 2009). In contrast, covert collections occur when firms gather data without the users' awareness, so companies monitor and track the users' online behavior without explicitly mentioning it to them (Xu, Luo, Carroll, & Rosson, 2011). The information gathered by these techniques can be used by the online merchant to personalize the users' online experience with features such as personalized advertisements or indices of product websites in order to enhance convenience and search efficiency (Laudon & Traver, 2008; Tam & Ho, 2006).

Despite the improved online experience, a conflict is prevailing with online personalization: Do the users want to share private information in order to get an automatically adapted web service or do they have too many concerns about the risk of losing anonymity online? Whether users want to share control of personal information to benefit from a personalized web experience can be described as a risk-value calculation. With an increasing number of data gathering companies, users' concerns for information privacy is on the rise. In a recent study, TRUSTe (2012) – the biggest online consumer advisor – found out that 91 percent of U.S. adults are worried about privacy online. Moreover, 53 percent do not disclose any personal information to businesses online because of mistrust. And further 88 percent tend to avoid firms that do not protect consumer privacy. Therefore, in order to get deeper insight into these privacy issues, more research has to focus on privacy concerns during the personalization process.

3 Conceptual Framework and Hypotheses

3.1 Privacy Concerns and CFIP

Since the landmark article 'The Right to Privacy' in 1890, in which privacy was formulated as "right to be let alone" (Warren & Brandeis, 1890, p. 193), almost every time a new technology with improved possibilities to capture, save, analyze and exchange detailed personal data emerged, privacy concerns soared (Culnan, 1993). This was particularly the case when web-based marketing occurred in 1995, which reduced the cost of gathering private information to a minimum (Laudon & Traver, 2008). Over time, the definition of privacy changed or got supplemented with extensions. One of these is information privacy, a subset of general privacy (Laudon & Traver, 2008). Recent definitions have focused on the users' ability to control the dissemination and use of their personal information (Phelps, Nowak, & Ferrell, 2000).

Smith et al. (1996) have developed the construct of concerns for information privacy (CFIP). It is a second- order, formative construct that consists of four dimensions: collection, unauthorized secondary use, improper access and errors (Van Slyke, Shim, Johnson, & Jiang, 2006). The first dimension deals with concerns about companies gathering personal information. The second item centers on concerns about the use of the gathered data for a secondary purpose that has not been authorized by the user. Improper access, the third factor, reflects the individual's concerns about gathered data being available for access to unauthorized third persons. Finally, the fourth dimension, errors, centers around the concerns about accuracy; that is, whether the gathered information really reflects the individuals (Smith, Milberg, & Burke, 1996).

Studies on the effect of privacy concerns and personalization have not included CFIP in their models. However, although research on the effects of CFIP in the context of e-commerce and personalization has been limited, many studies have focused on similar issues relevant to the given CFIP dimensions. The antecedent factors influencing CFIP that prior research has analyzed so far can be grouped into four categories: individual factors, social and legal norms, transaction and corporate factors, and information characteristics (Yuan, 2011). Research has also analyzed the consequences of privacy concerns. These literature findings can be grouped into beliefs, attitudes, intended and actual behavior (Yuan, 2011). A detailed overview of the prior research on CFIP and its findings can be found in appendix A and B. Summing up, privacy concerns influence human thoughts, opinions and actions. In general, privacy is seen as a precious good, which consumers value more than the disclosure of information. Connecting it to this study, CFIP should also influence users' perception of personalization: Personal values, such as privacy concerns, affect the value a user associates with the result of personalization (Awad & Krishnan, 2006). Therefore, a higher level of privacy concerns should result in a lower value of personalized service. Due to the nature of personalization, users have to give up a certain amount of privacy so that the merchant is able to adapt the offering to the individual taste (Chellappa & Sin, 2005). However, prior research has analyzed the effect of loss aversion, stating that people overvalue what they already have compared to things that they might attain (Novemsky & Kahneman, 2005). In other words, gains are valued less than losses. Hence, users should value advantages of personalization less than the lost personal privacy. Due to this, CFIP should have a negative impact on the value of personalization. More formally:

> H_1: Online user's Concerns for Information Privacy has a negative influence on Customer's Value of Online Personalization.

Not only the value of personalization but also the risks related to it are affected by CFIP. Several privacy related risks are related to e-commerce and personalization, so for example, risk of privacy loss due to data collection, risk of improper access via third parties or risk of unauthorized secondary use of the information (Van Slyke, Shim, Johnson, & Jiang, 2006). Hence, if concerns for information increase, users should experience more risk. The higher the individual's concerns about information privacy, the more risk is perceived during the personalization. Stated as hypothesis:

> H_2: Online user's Concerns for Information Privacy has a positive influence on Risk Beliefs of Online Personalization.

3.2 Control of Personal Data and CFIP

In current literature, privacy is widely perceived as the control of information. According to Sheehan and Hoy (2000), two dimensions determine the users' control of information privacy: awareness of information collection and information usage. While awareness simply refers to whether users know that private data is gathered about them, usage implies how and for what purpose the gathered data is being deployed. Surprisingly, research has never concentrated on the collection and use of data as antecedents influencing CFIP in the context of personalization. A deeper analysis will provide a better understanding of antecedents of CFIP and personalization in order to maximize user satisfaction and website opportunities.

3.3 Data Gathering Method – Overt and Covert Approach

Nowadays, the use of customer information is one of the most important success factors in e-business. Nevertheless, the challenge of accumulating these knowledge data in a way customers feel comfortable with is still prevalent (Awad & Krishnan, 2006). Personal information can be gathered in two methods: overt and covert, so with and without the knowledge of the user. Montgomery et al. (2009) defines this overt/covert approach as active (to inform him or to post direct questions to the consumer) and passive (to make inferences based on transaction, clickstream or e-mail data) learning about customers. The type of data gathering has a direct connection to the control of personal information data. Knowledge that a website is collecting information about users for personalization – so an overt approach – therefore is an elementary prerequisite for control. Contrariwise, if users do not know about the fact that data about them is being collected, users have no control of it.

Research that included an overt vs. covert approach in combination with online personalization has been very limited. Xu et al. (2009) analyzed in a study on personalized mobile marketing how covert or overt personalization influence the perceived benefits and risks of information disclosure. They find that personalization increases the perceived value of information disclosure through both collecting methods and that perceived risk [value] has a negative [positive] impact on the value of information disclosure. Most striking is that personalization is only positively related to perceived risk of information disclosure when the data is gathered covertly, because there was no significant increase in perceived risk in an overt state.

Simply telling the user about the data collection process might show similar results as privacy seals or privacy policies. Several studies found out that informing users about the way how the web-merchant deals with privacy helps to decrease privacy concerns (Andrade, Kaltcheva, & Weitz, 2002; Nam, Song, Lee, & Park, 2006; Wirtz, Lwin, & Williams, 2007). Informing the user about the data collection enables an active two-way communication between the merchant and the user, which is an important antecedent of trust (O'Malley, Patterson, & Evans, 1997; Pitta, Franzak, & Laric, 2003). By offering a pellucid, overt approach, it is ensured that users know about the data being gathered, feel more control of the gathering process and hence trust the web partner more. The website might be able to decrease the concerns, when letting users participate in the personalization process.

Furthermore, users might feel a loss of privacy and even harm or betrayal, when they find out that data about them was gathered without an agreement (Cespedes & Smith, 1993). A personalized interface is the result of this data gathering process, so the nature of personalization allows users to realize that the website gathered private information about them. Therefore, consumers might feel a breach of trust, if the website gathers data covertly and automatically shows a highly personalized interface, which results in higher privacy concerns (Montgomery & Smith, 2009).

To conclude, if the user knows about the gathering of his personal data, he can have an impact in the process, decide whether he wants to disclose his data, and should gain more control of the personalization. Therefore, the following hypotheses are introduced:

H_{3a}: Overt Data Collection has a positive impact on online user's Concerns for Information Privacy.

H_{3b}: Covert Data Collection has a negative impact on online user's Concerns for Information Privacy.

3.4 Use of Data – Authorized Primary Use or Unauthorized Secondary Use

The second dimension of users' control of information privacy is information usage (Sheehan & Hoy, 1999). Two key types of data usage exist: primary use and secondary use. Primary use of information can be defined as a company's use of the accumulated personal data to improve sales and customer services, inventory and personnel planning and other corporate operations, which has previously been authorized by the customer (Culnan, 1993). Secondary use represents the use of the same information for a different purpose than the original reason of collecting (Culnan, 1993). This is - in most cases - not authorized by the user. A reason why companies apply personal information to an unauthorized use is that they can gain a strategic advantage through an effective secondary use (Porter & Millar, 1985). Analyzing and managing customer data is a critical success factor for all e-businesses (Awad & Krishnan, 2006). Unauthorized secondary use can happen internally - within different departments of the data gathering company – or externally – disclosure of the personal data to a third party (Van Dyke, Midha, & Nemati, 2007). However, although differences between primary and secondary use of information are well-defined in theory, in practice this distinction is not always existent. Websites gather data to enhance the user's online experience, nevertheless, no general rules exist that regulate which methods advance and which debase the users' online experience (Sipior, Ward, & Mendoza, 2011).

Companies can even attain customer data from firms that specialize in gathering personal data or from online advertising networks like AdWords or DoubleClick (Laudon & Traver, 2008; Liao, Liu, & Chen, 2011). To get an idea of the dimensions, one needs to understand that an average U.S. resident is profiled in about 100 different databases (VanHoose, 2003). Furthermore, about one quarter of all websites participate in 'cookie sharing'[1] among companies (Sipior, Ward, & Mendoza, 2011). From a legal point of view, secondary use of information is valid and it is common use online to share data between firms (O'Malley, Patterson, & Evans, 1997). However, if customers realize that their private data is not kept confidential, trust declines and willingness to disclose information decreases (Pitta, Franzak, & Laric, 2003). This act of data collection can create an image of corporate 'dataveillance', which leads to increased privacy concerns (Ashworth & Free, 2006; Culnan, 1993; Foxman & Kilcoyne, 1993).

Furthermore, it is not only the release of private data that fosters privacy concerns, but the opportunistic behavior of companies: It is widely common that companies sell private information and make money on that data. Customers experience a misuse

[1] Cookies can be shared and combined with other cookies, public records, survey data on the basis of an individual's unique identification mean, for example the social security number.

of their private information, while not even getting a share of the earnings (Dinev & Hart, 2006). If new technology is applied opportunistically, personal privacy will be threatened, which can result in further anxieties and a feeling of unfair treatment (McCreary, 2008; Nowak & Phelps, 1992; Preston J. , 2004).

Another reason for increased privacy concerns refers to the user's control of data. When a user keeps his private data privately, he has total control. This situation changes if he discloses his data to a second party, nevertheless it is still obvious who has access to the data. However, it becomes more complicated to control the access and the use of the data, when a third party comes into play: The user can easily lose the overview which parties have access to his private data; moreover, the third party can even spread the information further. In this situation, the customer no longer has any control over his personal data because it is not transparent with whom the data has been shared. Hence, this process should result in higher privacy concerns.

Summing up, the more parties have unauthorized access to the user's private data, the more privacy concerns should evolve. Therefore, the following hypothesis can be formulated:

H_{4a}: Primary Use of Data has a negative impact on online user's Concerns for Information Privacy.

H_{4b}: Secondary Use of Data has a positive impact on online user's Concerns for Information Privacy.

3.5 Willingness to Transact

The Internet enables users to conduct a 'second exchange' (Li, Sarathy, & Xu, 2010), so consumers can decide to 'pay' with their personal data in order to acquire personalized products or services online. In this study, this decision is represented by the behavioral intention of users to participate in a personalization process. The dependent variable represents the user's wish to disclose private information to transact on the Internet. Using personalization, users are participating in a 'privacy calculus', so a cost-benefit analysis between value and risks of personalization (Malhotra, Kim, & Agarwal, Internet Users' Information Privacy Concerns (IUIPC): The Construct, the Scale, and a Causal Model, 2004; Li, Sarathy, & Xu, 2010; Xu, Zhang, Shi, & Song, 2009). Therefore, willingness to transact represents the individual's assessment of the utility of the information disclosure weighted against the potential risks. Customers will accept a loss of privacy, as long as a positive net result is achieved by the disclosure of their private information (Chellappa & Sin, 2005).

3.6 Customers' Value of Online Personalization

Individuals are likely to give up a degree of privacy, if they get something in return to compensate for it (Xu, Luo, Carroll, & Rosson, 2011). Moreover, the perceived value of the outcome of the information disclosure is potentially related to the willingness to give information. The value of online personalization and the advantages for users can be grouped in to three different categories: product, convenience and quality of service, and relationships. The most obvious advantage is the adapted product or service the online-company offers. It is aligned to meet the specific preferences and needs by incorporating the data the user supplied (Chellappa & Sin, 2005) and therefore offers a positive influence on willingness to transact. Ansari and Mela (2003) showed that click-through rates could be increased by 62 per cent when using personalized e-mails. The second group of advantages is convenience and quality of the related service: a personalized website decreases transaction and search time, because customer preferences are already known and do not have to be entered each time the customer returns to the website. This implies a more convenient service for the customer and perceived usefulness is increased (Davis, 1989; Hui, Teo, & Lee, 2007; Lee & Lee, 2009; Wolfinbarger & Gilly, 2001). Furthermore, the website will only provide online services, advertisements and recommendations that are relevant and anticipated for the user (Laudon & Traver, 2008; Phelps, Nowak, & Ferrell, 2000; Vesanen, 2007). Howard and Kerin (2004) found out that simply inserting the user's name in personalized product recommendations significantly increased the response rates. Hence, this process will increase the quality of decision making (Lee & Lee, 2009). The third group of benefits is relationship related: an interactive two-way communication is enabled and a relationship is created between the company and the customer (Rayport & Jaworski, 2003; Sheehan & Hoy, 2000; Smith, Milberg, & Burke, 1996). This connotes an intangible benefit for the customer, which reduces the perceived risk and offers an intrinsic social benefit of relationship participation (O'Malley, Patterson, & Evans, 1997). Summing up, it can be stated that personalization increases customer satisfaction and customer value at hand (Ariely, 2000; Montgomery & Smith, 2009; Turban, 2008; Vesanen, 2007). Therefore, the following hypothesis can be drawn:

H_5: Customers' Value of Online Personalization has a positive influence on the users' Willingness to Transact.

3.7 Risk Beliefs of Online Personalization

Risk evaluation and the fear of losing control over the collection, protection, and use of private information is always present online (Van Slyke, Shim, Johnson, & Jiang, 2006). Generally, risk can be defined as a subjective assessment of the possibility of loss (Dinev & Hart, 2006). In e-commerce, prior literature has identified three types of risks: economic risk, personal risk, and privacy risk (Van Slyke, Shim, Johnson, & Jiang, 2006). While economic risks concentrate on the potential monetary loss and personal risks focus on gaining insecure products or services or unsatisfying work results, privacy risks deal with the possible loss of private information or identity theft (Liao, Liu, & Chen, 2011). Research across different merchants, product types and cultures has been conducted on risks influence on willingness to engage in online transactions (Jarvenpaa, Tractinsky, & Vitale, 2000; Kimery & M. McCord, 2002; McKnight, Choudhury, & Kacmar, 2002). However, most of the studies focused on general risk or economic loss instead of the numerous sources of privacy risks, e.g. unwanted personalized advertisements, unauthorized access, or identity theft. Only a small number of studies have dealt with the influence of loss of privacy on the willingness to transact so far: Malhotra et al. (2004) found that risk beliefs have a negative impact on behavioral intentions; Li et al. (2010) proofed the same effect for privacy risk beliefs on behavioral intentions; Cocosila et al. (2009) analyzed that perceived privacy risk, mediated by perceived psychological risk, has a negative impact on behavioral intention to use; Van Slyke et al. (2006) showed a negative impact of risk perception on willingness to transact; Dinev and Hart (2006) found a negative influence of perceived Internet privacy risk on willingness to provide personal information to transact on the Internet. However, all of these studies did not analyze the risks concerned with online personalization. These can be classified into five categories: usability-, relationship-, monetary-, nonmonetary- and unauthorized use-related risks.

First, users are more or less compelled to disclose personal information, because some websites only work with restrictions or not at all if users do not register, which signifies problems with usability (Sipior, Ward, & Mendoza, 2011). Second, when users are aware of the fact that they are being monitored, they adapt their browsing behavior and avoid the publishing of sensitive information, which negatively influences the relationship between the two parties (Hui, Teo, & Lee, 2007; Laudon & Traver, 2008). Moreover, customers could even get aggressive and be incited to retaliation behavior, if they feel threatened or harmed (McCreary, 2008; Lee & Lee, 2009). Third, consumers can be confronted with monetary drawbacks, because firms might demand extra fees for personalizing the content (Vesanen, 2007). Fourth, users are concerned about the loss or misuse of nonmonetary goods and valuables, in connection to personalization, the loss of privacy or sensible data (Malhotra, Kim, & Agarwal, 2004). Concerns about loss of privacy are the most salient reason of denial to establish a relationship with merchants (Dinev & Hart, 2006; Liao, Liu, & Chen, 2011; Phelps, D'Souza, & Nowak, 2001). Fifth, the risk of unauthorized use like identity thefts via spyware or hacker attacks is constantly present (Chaffey, 2007; Heffes, 2005; McCreary, 2008; Pitta, Franzak, & Laric, 2003). All these risks can stimulate fear of loss of privacy in the user´s mind (Lee & Lee, 2009). Users should therefore be reluctant to disclose private information and their willingness to transact with a personalized website should decrease. More formally stated:

H_6: Risk Beliefs of Online Personalization have a negative influence on user's Willingness to Transact.

3.8 Perceived Usefulness of Online Personalization

Similar to willingness to transact, value and risk should also influence the perceived usefulness of personalization. Perceived usefulness describes the users' impression whether personalization improves their online experience, so in this context, whether it makes online shopping more effective, quick or convenient. This means the difference between the value of personalization and the usefulness of it lies in the specific, relevant benefits of the personalization for the consumer in this scenario. While the construct for Consumers' Value of Online Personalization measures the consumers' attitude to personalization in general, the Usefulness of Online Personalization construct measures the applicability and relevance of personalization to the specific online shopping scenario. Hence, it is hypothesized that, if users value personalization in general, the perceived usefulness for the online shopping task will be higher. Otherwise, if users fear the risks of personalization more, perceived usefulness will decrease. More formally:

H_7: Customers' Value of Online Personalization has a positive influence on the users' Perceived Usefulness of Personalization.

H_8: Risk Beliefs of Online Personalization have a negative influence on user's Perceived Usefulness of Personalization.

Marketers wish to deliver a product or service that is automatically adapted to the specific individual needs of the customers. However, for this concept, it is necessary that users realize the advantages offered by personalization. If the personalization application is not helpful and makes the interaction with the website less convenient, then users do not perceive it as useful. Nunes and Kambli (2001) present the results of a survey, in which only around six percent of online users would prefer personalization compared to customization. The reason for this is, with customization, users can adapt the product or service to their needs if a need for change exists, and make it more relevant for them. In personalization however, this option is not given. Lee & Lee (2009) found a large positive influence of usefulness of personalization on customers' intention to use. Hence, if perceived usefulness of personalization already is high, users should be more willing to transact. Alternatively, if personalization is redundant, users' willingness to use the service should be low. Hence, personalization has to be useful, convenient and especially relevant for online users. Therefore, the following hypothesis can be formulated:

H_9: Perceived Usefulness of Personalization has a positive influence on user's Willingness to Transact..

3.9 Moderating Role of Trust Beliefs between Use of Data and CFIP

Similar to the offline world, relationships rely on trust, commitment and mutual benefits (Morgan & Hunt, 1994; O'Malley, Patterson, & Evans, 1997). Furthermore, successful relationship building requires the processing of information (O'Malley, Patterson, & Evans, 1997). Trust has been found to affect the attitude a consumer has towards a merchant (Moorman, Zaltman, & Deshpande, 1992). More specifically, trust being closely related to privacy is a crucial element for transactions that involve risk, so for example online transactions (Kim, Tao, Shin, & Kim, 2010; McKnight, Choudhury, & Kacmar, 2002; Reichheld & Schefter, 2000). This paper defines trusting beliefs as confidence that the firm deals responsibly with the collected customer data. This means that if trust in the online merchant is high, users should expect that merchants use the information gathered in a sensible and intelligent way. Hence, the more trust the user has in the website, the more positive will be his evaluation of secondary use of information. If the user trusts the merchant to prevent opportunistic behavior and to strive for a mutual benefit, then he could even perceive the secondary use of information as an extra personalization service by the merchant. In other words, people may trust in the merchant's ability to decide over secondary use of information for the user's welfare.

Furthermore, people disclose more information about themselves if they trust in the addressee (Pitta, Franzak, & Laric, 2003). This can be traced back to fewer risk beliefs, which users perceive, when trusting a merchant. Prior studies found out that trust can reduce concerns of disclosing personal information and increase willingness to transact (Liu, Marchewka, Lu, & Yu, 2005). Opposing to this, if the user does not trust the merchant and finds that data is illegitimately shared with a third party, this perception of misuse of his private data can even increase privacy concerns and decrease his willingness to transact (Liao, Liu, & Chen, 2011; Pitta, Franzak, & Laric, 2003). Therefore, the following hypothesis is stated:

H_{10}: Trust Beliefs in the Online Merchant moderate the relationship between Use of Data and Concerns for Information Privacy.

The conceptual model and the hypotheses are visualized in Figure 1. The next section of the paper will present the conducted research and the results.

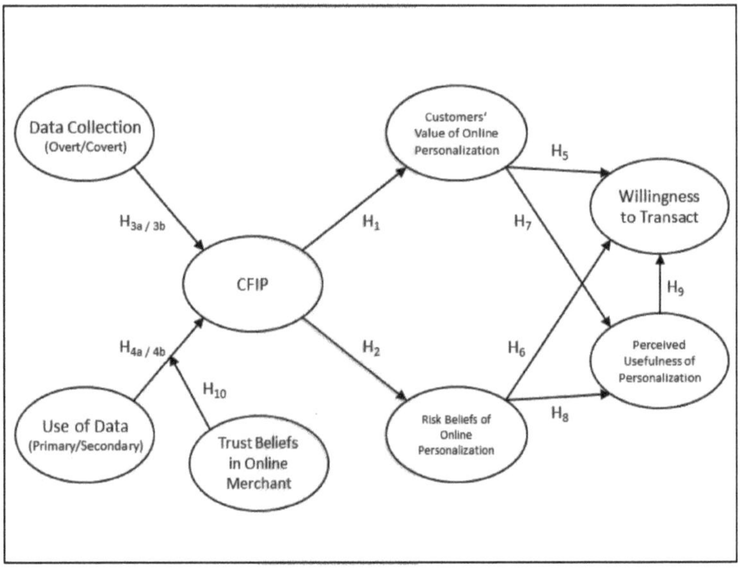

Figure 1 - Conceptual Model and Hypotheses

4 Research Design and Results

To test the hypotheses of the conceptual framework, an online survey was developed and conducted amongst a sample of Amazon Mechanical Turk. Next, the data collection process, sample, questionnaire design, and measurement instruments will be discussed in detail.

4.1 Data Collection Process

Before the final data collection, a pre-test with 56 Mechanical Turk users was conducted, to ensure respondents understood the different scenarios and that the manipulations work correctly. The analysis of these responses showed that participants had a clear understanding of the respective scenario they read that the scenarios were evaluated realistically and easy imagine. A significant difference between the different scenario groups was observed.

4.2 Sample Description

A sample of 186 responses was obtained by recruiting participants via Amazon Mechanical Turk. This is a web service that works as an online panel, by linking researches and individual participants. Recent research states that Mechanical Turk samples bring similar results as using college students and urban samples (e.g., Fagerlin et al., 2007; Oppenheimer, Meyvis, & Davidenko, 2009). However, 23 responses had to be deleted because of not completely filling out the questionnaire and one outlier in CFIP was removed. After cleaning the data, 162 complete surveys remained. Participants completed all procedures online. Of these respondents, 40.5% are male. The age of the participants were grouped as follows: 17.8% were 18-24, 33.7% were 25-34, 17.2% were 35-44, 22.1% were 45-54, 5.5% were 55-64, and 3.7% were 65 years old or older. In terms of education, the following distribution was obtained: 1,8% had some school education but no degree, 12.9% had a high school degree, 38.0 had some college education but no college degree, 33.1% had a Bachelor's degree, 8.6% had a Master's degree, 1.8% a professional degree, and 3.7% had a doctorate degree.

4.3 Questionnaire Design

The design of the questionnaire was divided into seven sections. It started with a section testing the trust beliefs regarding the online merchant. After that, participants were randomly assigned to one of the four different scenarios, so a 2 (Data Collection: overt vs. covert) x 2 (Use of Data: primary vs. secondary use) design was used. To manipulate the conditions, participants were asked to put themselves into a fictional character who bought a DVD online at the online merchant Best Buy. In the overt data collection condition, participants were informed that Best Buy gathers and saves customer information to improve their personalization services, while in the covert condition this text was replaced by a standard text that promoted free shipping and the customer service hotline. Then, all groups were told that a week later, they saw personalized advertisements and recommendations online. In the primary use condition, this was displayed on the Best Buy homepage, while for the secondary use condition, the third party retailer Amazon was used. Images of the used manipulations can be found in appendix C. This manipulation process was followed by the measures of the CFIP construct. This was followed by sections for the value and risk beliefs of online personalization and, after that, two sections for usefulness of online personalization and willingness to transact appeared. The questionnaire ended with the more sensitive covariate questions for gender, age and education.

4.4 Measures

In order to measure the relevant constructs of the previously specified conceptual framework, established scales from prior literature were used. These scales were adapted in terms of wording to fit the specific online personalization scenario context. All items were seven-point likert scales, anchored from strongly disagree to strongly agree. A detailed overview of the measurement constructs can be found in Appendix C. CFIP was measured by Van Slyke et al.'s (2006) second-order construct with four dimensions: collection (4 items), errors (4 items), unauthorized access (3 items), and secondary use (4 items), which is based on the original developed scale of Smith et al. (1996). To measure customer's value of online personalization, the six item construct of Chellappa and Sin (2005) was applied. Regarding risk beliefs of online personalization, a four item construct of Malhotra et al. (2004) was used. Willingness to transact was measured by a three item measure of Van Slyke et al (2006) and for usefulness of personalization a five item scale by Tam & Ho (2006) was utilized. To measure the estimated moderating variable trust belief in the online merchant, a three item construct by Malhotra et al. (2004) was used. Finally, the questionnaire contained some questions on respondents' socio-demographics. Respondents were asked to indicate their gender, age and education category.

4.5 Scale Validity and Reliability

All previous introduced constructs are reflective, since the manifest items are highly correlated and the meaning of the constructs would not change if an individual item was removed (Jarvis, MacKenzie, & Podsakoff, 2003). The internal consistency of the model is measured by Cronbach's alpha (Nunnally, 1978). Additionally, a measure of composite reliability was used, which is according to Chin (1998) more reliable, because it is not affected by the number of indicators used in the construct. A detailed summary of the results is given in Figure 2. All scales meet the recommended threshold criterion and exceed the value of 0.7 for both measures (Nunnally, 1978). Convergent validity is tested by examining the factor loadings and the average variance extracted (AVE). All items load significantly (>0.70) on their posited underlying constructs, except one (Item 6 of Value). However, this item loads with a value greater than 0.6, which is still an acceptable result (Malhotra, 2010). Furthermore, all AVE scores are greater than 0.50, so convergent validity is given (Fornell & Larcker, 1981). Discriminant validity is checked for by applying the Fornell and Larcker criterion (1981). For all constructs, the square root of AVE exceeds the constructs correlations with all other constructs, showing the measures' discriminant validity.

Construct		CR	Cronbach's Alpha
CFIP	Collection	0.955	0.937
	Access	0.949	0.919
	Error	0.954	0.936
	Use	0.878	0.816
Customers' Value of Online Personalization		0.912	0.885
Risk Belief of Online Personalization		0.956	0.939
Usefulness of Online Personalization		0.975	0.968
Willingness to Transact		0.966	0.947
Trust Belief in Online Merchant		0.922	0.874

Figure 2 - Convergent Validity and Cronbach's Alpha

4.6 Data Analysis and Results

In order to test the conceptual model, structural equation modeling (SEM) was conducted with a 900 subsample bootstrapping procedure with a Warp3 PLS regression algorithm (Kock, 2012). PLS is an appropriate method to test the hypothesized models because PLS is a well suited technique for exploratory and confirmatory research endeavors as well as theory development (Hair, Ringle, & Sarstedt, 2011; Marcoulides & Saunders, 2006).

4.7 Model Evaluation

The R^2 values of the construct to examine the explanatory power of the predictor variable(s) are reported in Figure 3. Jointly, Data Collection and Use of Data predict 4.6% of the Concerns for Information Privacy. Tests for an interaction effect between the two independent variables showed no significant results ($F(3,150) = 0,953$, $p = 0.330$). CFIP explains 8.5% of Customers' Value of Online Personalization and 29.2% of the Risk Beliefs of Online Personalization. Furthermore, Customers' Value of Online Personalization and Risk Beliefs of Online Personalization together predict 39.7% of Perceived Usefulness of Personalization.

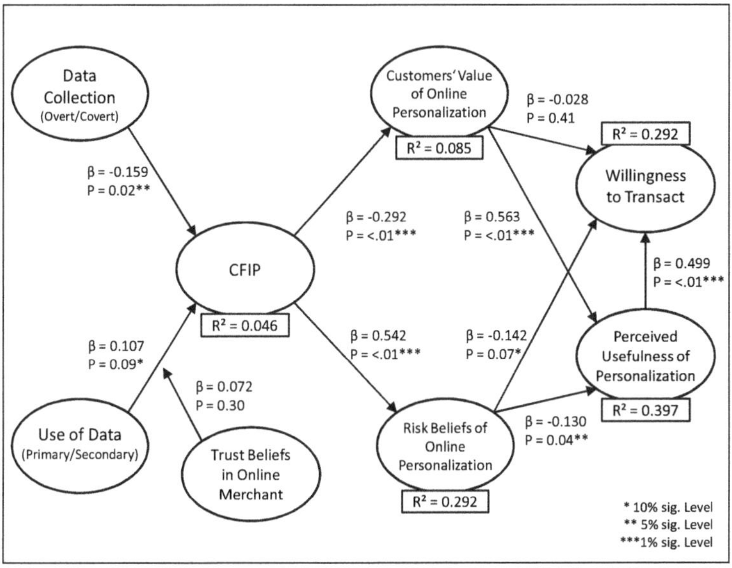

Figure 3 - Main Effects and Path Coefficients

Finally, Customers' Value of Online Personalization, Risk Beliefs of Online Personalization and Perceived Usefulness of Personalization explain 29.2% of Willingness to Transact. Additionally, further conceptual models were tested, which left out different constructs. These can be found in Appendix E. However, the R^2 values were in nearly all cases not as high as in the featured conceptual model, so no further analysis was conducted with them.

WarpPLS offers three measures to access the model fit: average path coefficient (APC), average R-squared (ARS), and average variance inflation factor (AVIF). For APC and ARS, Kock suggests a 0.05 significance criterion for the p-values and for AVIF a value lower than 5. With p<.001 (APC = <.001; ARS = <.001) for the two first two measures and an AVIF with 1.251, all criteria fulfill the requirements. Furthermore, Tenenhaus (2005) recommends calculating a goodness of fit (GoF) indicator, so the global fit of the model can be accessed. The measure ($GoF = \sqrt{\overline{\text{AVE}} * \overline{\text{R}^2}}$) uses the geometric mean of the average communality and the average R^2 (for endogenous constructs). Wetzels, Odekerken-Schröder and van Oppen (2009) suggest the following cut-off criteria for assessing the results of the GoF measurement: Gofsmall = 0.1; GoF medium = 0.25; GoF large = 0.36. For the complete model a GoF value of 0.48 was obtained, which indicates a very good overall model fit.

4.8 Main Effects and Path Coefficients

The following analysis deals with the main effects of the proposed model. Figure 3 shows the path coefficients, the respective significance levels and the coefficients of determination. All effect sizes were accessed with Hensler & Chins's (2010) criterion (>0.02 = weak, >0.15 = moderate, >0.35 = strong). In line with hypotheses H1, CFIP has a medium, negative impact on Customer's Value of Online Personalization. Precisely, a one-standard deviation increase in CFIP leads to the weak effect of a 29.2% standard deviation decrease in customer's value ($f^2 = 0.085$, p = <.01). Furthermore, in line with H2, CFIP have a moderate, positive influence on Risk Beliefs of Online Personalization. Per one-standard deviation increase in concerns for information privacy risk beliefs increased by 54.2% ($f^2 = 0.294$, p = <.01). Contrary to the hypothesis 3a and 3b, it was found that concerns were lower when data was collected covertly and higher when consumers were informed about the collection process. In detail, when the data was collected covertly, concerns decreased weakly by 15.9% ($f^2 = 0.026$, p = 0.02). To examine the manipulation effects in more detail, a two-way between groups ANOVA was conducted to check for potential interaction effects (Data Collection*Use of Data). However, the interaction effect did not reach statistical significance ($F(3, 158) = 1.83$, p = 0.178). Hypotheses H4a and H4b were confirmed because Use of Data had a significant effect on CFIP at a .10 sig. level (f^2 = 0.013, p = 0.09). In detail, when data was used for secondary, unauthorized purposes CFIP increased by 10.7%. Furthermore, H5 was not confirmed. Customer's Value of Online Personalization has no significant influence on Willingness to transact. A one-standard deviation increase of the former just triggers a 2.8% (f^2 = 0.009, p = 0.41) standard deviation rise in willingness to transact. However, hypothesis 6 was confirmed at a .10 sig. level. Risk Beliefs of Online Personalization caused a weak decrease of willingness to transact by 14.2% (f^2 = 0.040, p = 0.07). In line with hypothesis H7, Customer's Value of Online Personalization has a strong positive influence on Perceived Usefulness of Personalization. Per one-standard deviation increase of value perceived usefulness rises by 56.3% (f^2 = 0.349, p = <.01). Hypothesis H8 was also confirmed: Risk Beliefs of Online Personalization has a small negative influence on Perceived Usefulness of Online Personalization. Precisely, a one-standard deviation increase in risk beliefs weakly triggered a 13.0% (f^2 = 0.048, p = 0.04) decrease in perceived usefulness. Finally, hypothesis H9 was confirmed as well, since Perceived Usefulness of Personalization has a medium, positive influence on Willingness to Transact. More accurately, a one-standard deviation increase in perceived usefulness leads to a moderate, 49.9% increase in users' willingness to transact (f^2 = 0.261, p = <.01).

4.9 Indirect Effects

The effects of several variables as potential mediators were examined. Several indirect effects were found and are reported below. First, Data Collection has - beside its main effect – three significant indirect effects at a 5% significance level: on Customers' Value of Online Personalization (β = 0.046, f^2 = 0.001), Risk Beliefs of Online Personalization (β = -0.086, f^2 = 0.005), and Perceived Usefulness of Online Personalization (β = 0.037,

$f^2 = 0.002$). The Use of Data influences shows one indirect effect on Risk Beliefs of Online Personalization ($\beta = 0.097$, $f^2 = 0.006$) at a 10% sig. level. For CFIP, two indirect effects were identified at a 1% level: on Willingness to Transact ($\beta = -0.186$, $f^2 = 0.035$) and Perceived Usefulness ($\beta = -0.235$, $f^2 = 0.073$). Furthermore, Customers' Value of Online Personalization has an indirect effect at a 10% sig. level on Willingness to Transact ($\beta = 0.281$, $f^2 = 0.093$). Finally, Risk Beliefs of Online Personalization triggers an indirect effect at a 5% significance level on Willingness to Transact ($\beta = -0.065$, $f^2 = 0.018$).

4.10 Moderation Analysis

The effects of Trust Beliefs in Online Merchant as potential moderators on the relationship between Use of Data and Concerns For Information Privacy was examined. In this context, an interaction term was created. However, H10 is not confirmed, since trust beliefs in the online merchant do not significantly moderate the relationship between Use of Data and CFIP ($f^2 = 0.007$, $p = 0.30$).

5 Discussion and Conclusion

5.1 Theoretical Implications

The current study is the first to establish a link between different types of data collection, different use purposes and concerns for information privacy in the context of personalization. Furthermore, it analyses the consequences of varying CFIP on customers' value of personalization and involved risk beliefs, and consecutively on perceived usefulness and willingness to transact.

In detail, the results show that privacy concerns increase when the online merchant informs users about gathering personal and/or behavioral information about its customers. This shows that being honest with best intentions, in this case indicating customers about intrusion of their privacy, does not show similar results like privacy seals or policies (Nam, Song, Lee, & Park, 2006; Wirtz, Lwin, & Williams, 2007), but instead, triggers concerns about privacy. The attempt to lower privacy concerns by informing users has provoked a contrary effect, so calling their attention for data collection and increasing their concerns by doing this. In addition to that, fully mediated, indirect effect of covert data collection on value, users' perceived usefulness and risk beliefs of personalization were observed. This proves the strong impact of the data collection method within the given conceptual model.

The use of the gathered data also has a significant influence on concerns. Like hypothesized, when the data is shared with a third party - which is one example of an unauthorized, secondary use - consumers experience a misuse of their data, which raises privacy concerns. Moreover, data collection has a completely mediated, positive influence on risk beliefs. Hence, the feeling of losing control over the data clearly increases concerns and risks likewise.

Additionally, concerns for information privacy decrease the value of personalization and increase risk beliefs that people feel when personalization is applied. The more users are concerned, the less value they see in the advantages of personalization and the more risk is perceived. Also, a similar result like Malhotra et al. (2004) for the influence of CFIP on the behavioral intention was found: concerns have no indirect influence on perceived usefulness and willingness to transact, but its effects are completely mediated by the value and risks of personalization.

The value of personalization only has an indirect effect via perceived usefulness on willingness to transact, connoting a partial mediation. If users judge personalization in general and its applicability in the specific scenario positively, then their willingness to interact with the website increases. The risk beliefs, which users experience when dealing with personalization, negatively influences the willingness to transact directly, as well as indirectly, partially mediated by perceived usefulness of personalization. Another finding is that, if personalization is perceived as useful, convenient and relevant for the task at hand, then users are more willing to transact.

Finally, the study showed that trust in the web merchant does not moderate the relationship between the use of the data and the related concerns for information privacy. Users are still concerned if personal data is shared with a third party, even if their trust in the online shop is high.

5.2 Managerial Implications

From a practical perspective, the results stress the importance of effective communication about data collection, data use and concerns about online privacy. Today, it is essential for companies to form long-term relationships with customers offline as well as online (Pitta, Franzak, & Laric, 2003). Companies should talk to consumers to find out how to communicate privacy policies best and where to draw the line between additional services and intrusion into privacy. The Internet and particularly personalization are tools that help to enable active two-way communication in order to fulfill this goal. As personalization requires personal data, firms have to collect it in a way users feel comfortable with and at the same time make efficient use of it. Due to the results of this study, firms should try to stick to well-known concern-reducing techniques, such as privacy statements or seals, to establish high-quality relationships with customers, instead of using a pellucid but simple approach of informing customers directly. Besides, data should not be used opportunistically or for an unauthorized secondary use. Businesses should care about privacy and users' concerns because it is directly linked to customers' perception of the service and their willingness to transact. Managers should think beyond existing rules to values, anticipate privacy issues, create accountability and make plans for a disaster recovery. Furthermore, the results show that trust in the online merchant cannot eradicate the negative influence of unauthorized secondary use. Hence, marketers should weigh the pros and cons of new applications carefully even when customers highly trust in the online merchant. The study also confirms that if companies decide to invest in personalization instead of the cheaper alternative of static content (Hagel & Rayport, 1997), it has to be useful and relevant for the specific task at hand. If this is the case, more users are willing to accept the risks of personalization.

5.3 Limitations and Future Research

This study has several limitations, which should be considered when evaluating the results. However, these limitations also provide interesting possibilities for future research. First, the analysis was conducted with a sample obtained from the crowdsourcing internet marketplace Amazon Mechanical Turk and the data collected for this study was specific to a given geographic location (i.e., the United States). Although an MTurk sample reflects a good cross section of society (Ipeirotis, 2010), participants are voluntary, Internet-savvy individuals. Therefore, care must be taken in any effort to generalize these findings beyond the boundary of our sample. Second, it must be taken into account that the respondents had to put themselves into a hypothetical scenario. Asking participants direct questions about privacy might lead to biased responses because people might (over-)emphasize their concerns. The results may not reflect the true attitude towards privacy concerns, so interpretation must be done carefully. Third, the study did not examine actual behavior but perceived estimations and behavioral intentions. The measured constructs are theoretical and although behavioral intentions can be judged as reliable predictor of actual behavior (Ajzen, 1991), the presented framework should be reexamined with an additional measure of actual user behavior. Furthermore, it is to be noted that correlation does not imply causality. Fourth, users' reactions to a specific privacy threat are highly dependent on the scenario and contextual factors. It has to be analyzed whether the findings are also valid with different contextual variables, e.g. different personalization methods or other forms of secondary use. Furthermore, two well-known online merchants were used for the scenario, so privacy concerns might be specific about these retailers or prior concerns might have existed before the manipulation. These limitations have to be taken into account when interpreting the results. Fifth, other factors that were not measured in this study, like familiarity with the Internet or prior negative experiences with information misuse, might have influenced the results and must be thought of when analyzing the results.

The opportunities for future research are fourfold. For example, this study analyses only two types of beliefs in the context of information privacy and personalization - namely, value of online personalization and risk beliefs. Yet, it is possible that other forms of beliefs also play an important role in consumer behavior. For example, humans are likely to perceive injustice if they are not satisfied with a marketer's information practices or when user data is shared with a third party. It would be worth to investigate whether a feeling of injustice influences the results. Furthermore, research has to gain a deeper understanding about personalization. Of particular importance here is to find out how to determine the right level of personalization, in which participants perceive more value gained than privacy lost. This could help marketers to plan investments and ROI more efficiently. Besides personalization, privacy concerns are still not completely understood. Exemplary research aspects are whether privacy concerns vary over time or what the most abhorrent privacy concerns are. A better understanding of privacy concerns would thus help researches and marketers alike.

Appendices

Appendix A: Antecedents of CFIP

Category	Construct	Item	Effect on CFIP	Authors
Individual factors	Demographhc influences	Gender	Women more concerned than mei	Fogel & Nehmad, 2009; Hoy & Milne, 2010; Joinson et al., 2010
		Age	Positive impact	Joinson et al., 2010; Laric, Pitta & Katsanis, 2008
		Education	No influence	Chen, Yue & Heath, 2001; Ji & Lieber, 2010
		Income	No influence	Chen, Yue & Heath, 2001; Ji & Lieber, 2010
	Personality traits	Paranoia	Positive impact	Smith, Milberg & Burke,1996
		Social Criticism	Positive impact	Smith, Milberg & Burke,1996
		Cynical Distrust	Positive impact	Smith, Milberg & Burke,1996
		Social Awareness	Positive impact	Smith, Milberg & Burke,1996
	Prior knowledge and online experience	Previous experience with information misuse and disclosure	Positive impact	Smith, Milberg & Burke,1996
		Knowledge of media coverage on information misuse	Positive impact	Smith, Milberg & Burke,1996
		Previous experience with online privacy inversion	Positive impact	Bansal, Zahedi & Gefen, 2010
		Internet literacy	Negative impact*	Dinev & Hart, 2006
		Internet experience	Negative impact*	Bellman et al., 2004
		Web usage	Positive impact*	Zviran, 2008
		Use of privacy enhancing mechanisms	Positive impact*	Zviran, 2008
		Web skills	No impact*	Janda & Fair, 2004
		Web experience	No impact*	Janda & Fair, 2004
	Psychological factors	Psychological need for privacy	Positive impact	Yao, Rice & Wallis, 2007
		Beliefs in privacy rights on online privacy concerns	Positive impact	Yao, Rice & Wallis, 2007
		Computer anxiety	Positive impact	Stewart & Segars, 2002
		Perceived control	Negative impact	Xu et al., 2008
		Perceived Internet privacy risks	Positive impact	Dinev & Hart, 2006; Xu et al., 2008
		Trust beliefs	Negative impact	Pavlou, Huigang & Yajiong, 2007
Social and legal norms	Social norms	Power distance	Positive impact	Milberg et al., 2008
		Individualism	Positive impact	Milberg et al., 2008
		Masculinity	Positive impact	Milberg et al., 2008
		Uncertainty avoidance	Negative impact	Milberg et al., 2008
	Legal norms	Absence of governmental privacy regulations	Positive impact	Bellman et al., 2004
Transaction and corporate factors		Privacy policy	Negative impact	Andrade, Kaltcheva & Weitz, 2002; Nam et al., 2006
		Third party assurance	Negative impact	Andrade, Kaltcheva & Weitz, 2002; Nam et al., 2006
		Company's reputation	Negative impact	Eastlick, Lotz & Warrington, 2006
		Company's trustworthiness	Negative impact	Andrade, Kaltcheva & Weitz, 2002
Information Characteristics	Types of Information	Gathering different types of information	Mixed results	Ji & Lieber, 2010; Ward, Bridges & Chitty, 2005: Zimmer et al., 2010
	Information Sensitivity	Sensitive information	Positive impact	Malhotra et al., 2004

*similar item, but ambivalent results

Appendix B: Consequences of CFIP

Category	Construct	CFIP's Effect	Authors
Personal Beliefs	Trust Beliefs	Negative impact	e.g. Bansal, Zahedi & Gefen, 2010; Malhotra et al. 2004; Lu & Yu, 2005
	Risk Beliefs	Positive impact	e.g. Cocosila, Archer & Yuan, 2009; Malhotra et al. 2004; Van Slyke et al., 2006
Attitudes	Attitude towards a website	Positive impact	Cases et al., 2010
	Comfort to share information	Positive impact	Frye & Dornisch, 2010
	Customer relationship program receptiveness	Negative impact	Ashley et al., 2011
Behavioral Intention	Willingness to share information	Negative impact	Dinev & Hart, 2006; Eastlick, Lotz & Warrington, 2006; Smith, Milberg & Burke, 1996
	Intention to protect information	Positive impact	Dinev & Hart, 2006; Eastlick, Lotz & Warrington, 2006; Smith, Milberg & Burke, 1996
Actual Behavior	Refusal to provide personal information	Positive impact	Son & Kim, 2008
	Removal of information	Positive impact	Son & Kim, 2008
	Negative word-of-mouth	Positive impact	Son & Kim, 2008
	Complaining behavior to the company	Positive impact	Son & Kim, 2008
	Complaining behavior to third-parties	Positive impact	Son & Kim, 2008

Appendix C: Manipulations

Overt condition:

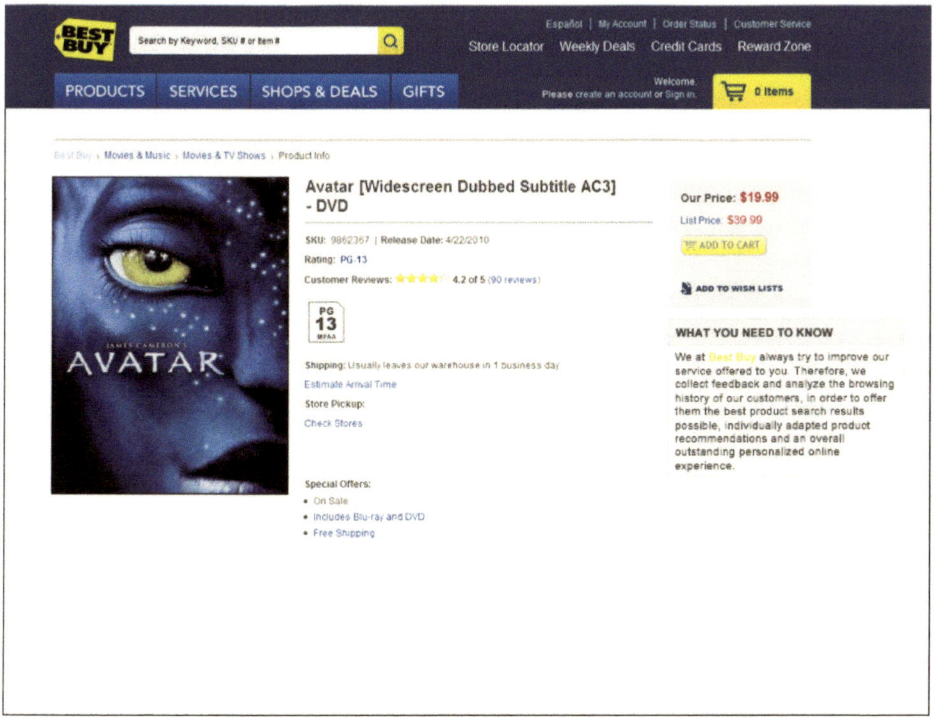

(BestBuy.com, 2012)

Covert condition:

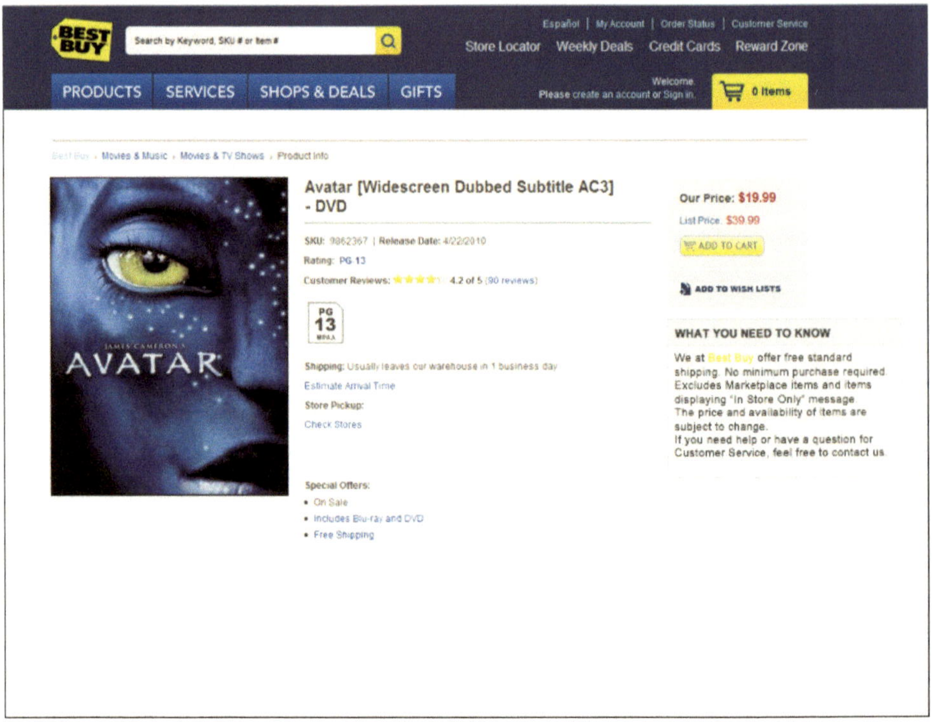

(BestBuy.com, 2012)

Primary Use:

(BestBuy.com, 2012)

Secondary Use:

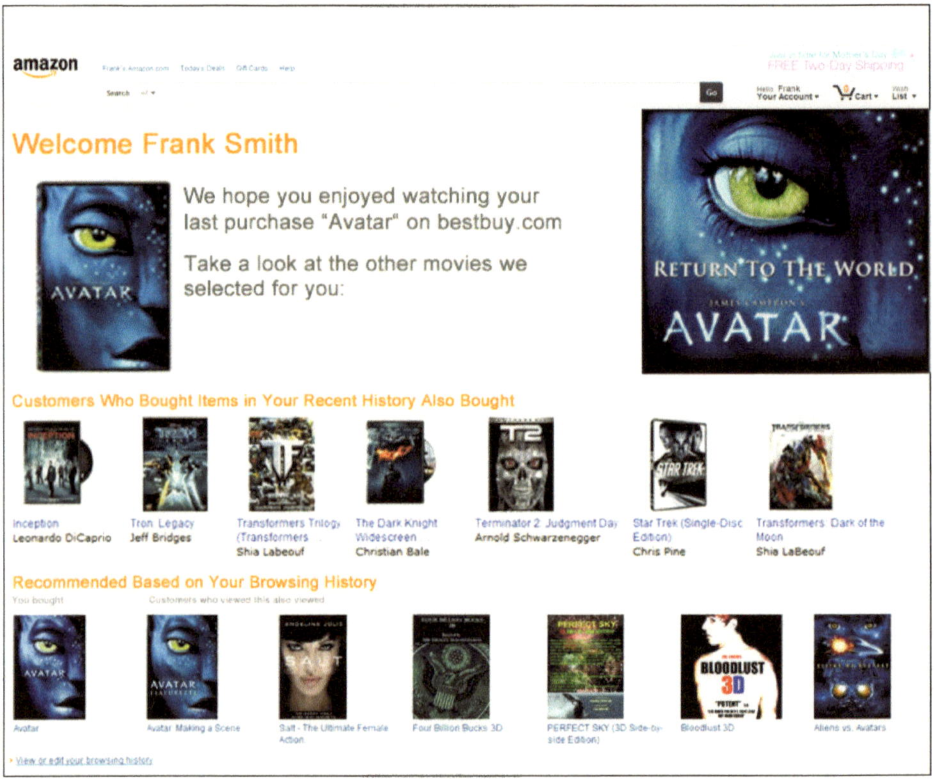

(Amazon.com, 2012)

Appendix D: Measurement Constructs

Construct	Authors	Item Wording	Cronbach's Alpha	Factor Loading	Composite Reliability	AVE
CFIP	(Van Slyke et al., 2006)					
Collection			0.94		0.96	0.84
Item 1		It would bother me if Best Buy asks me for personal information.		0.91		
Item 2		If Best Buy asks me for personal information, I would think twice before providing it.		0.90		
Item 3		It would bother me to give personal information to so many online companies, like Best Buy.		0.94		
Item 4		I'm concerned that Best Buy would be collecting too much personal information about me.		0.92		
Improper Access			0.92		0.95	0.86
Item 1		Best Buy should devote time and effort to preventing unauthorized access to personal information.		0.91		
Item 2		Computer databases that contain personal information should be protected from unauthorized access - no matter how much it costs.		0.93		
Item 3		Best Buy should take steps to make sure that unauthorized people cannot access personal information in their computers.		0.95		
Errors			0.94		0.95	0.84
Item 1		All the personal information in computer databases should be double-checked for accuracy by Best Buy - no matter how much this costs.		0.90		
Item 2		Best Buy should take steps to make sure that the personal information in their files is accurate.		0.95		
Item 3		Best Buy should have procedures to correct errors in personal information.		0.90		
Item 4		Best Buy should devote time and effort to verifying the accuracy of the personal information in their databases.		0.92		
Unauthorized Secondary Use			0.82		0.88	0.65
Item 1		Best Buy should not use personal information for any purpose unless it has been authorized by the individuals who provided information.		0.87		
Item 2		When people give personal information to an online company (e.g. Best Buy) for some reason, it should never use the information for any other reason.		0.81		
Item 3		Best Buy should never sell the personal information in their computer databases to other companies.		0.78		
Item 4		Best Buy should never share personal information with other companies unless it has been authorized by the individuals who provided the information.		0.76		
Consumers' Value of Online Personalization	(Chellappa, 2005)		0.89		0.91	0.64
Item 1		I would value if a Web page is personalized for the device (e.g. computer, mobile phone etc.), browser (e.g. Firefox, Internet explorer) and operating system (e.g. Windows, Mac) that I use.		0.76		
Item 2		I would value if a Web page is personalized for my usage experience preferences.		0.89		
Item 3		I would value if a Web page acquires my personal preferences and personalize the services and products themselves.		0.87		
Item 4		I would value if goods and services are personalized based on information that is collected automatically (such as IP address, pages viewed, access time) but cannot identify me as an individual.		0.79		
Item 5		I would value if goods and services are personalized based on information that I have voluntarily given out (such as age range, salary range, Zip Code) but cannot identify me as an individual.		0.81		
Item 6		I would value if goods and services are personalized based on information I have voluntarily given out and can identify me as an individual (such as name, shipping address, credit card information).		0.67		
Risk Beliefs of Online Personalization	(Malhotra et al., 2004)		0.94		0.96	0.85
Item 1		In general, it would be risky to give personal information for personalization purposes to a Web page like Best Buy.		0.91		
Item 2		There would be high potential for loss associated with giving personal information for personalization purposes to a Web page like Best Buy.		0.92		
Item 3		There would be too much uncertainty associated with giving personal information for personalization purposes to a Web page like Best Buy.		0.95		
Item 4		Providing a Web page like Best Buy with private information for personalization purposes would involve many unexpected problems.		0.90		
Trust Belief	(Malhotra et al., 2004)		0.97		0.98	0.89
Item 1		I trust that Best Buy would keep my best interests in mind when dealing with my personal information.		0.95		
Item 2		Best Buy is in general predictable and consistent regarding the usage of my personal information.		0.95		
Item 3		Best Buy is always honest with customers when it comes to using personal information that I would provide.		0.96		
Willingness to Transact	(Slyke et al., 2006)		0.95		0.97	0.90
Item 1		I intend on using Best Buy for some of my future purchases.		0.88		
Item 2		I am inclined to purchase Best Buy's goods.		0.89		
Item 3		I am likely to utilize the goods provided by Best Buy.		0.91		
Perceived Usefulness of Personalization	(Tam & Ho, 2006)		0.88		0.92	0.80
Item 1		Shopping with personalized product recommendations from Best Buy would enable me to accomplish shopping tasks more quickly.		0.91		
Item 2		Using personalized product recommendations from Best Buy would improve my shopping task performance.		0.95		
Item 3		Best Buy's personalized recommendations would enhance my effectiveness in my shopping tasks.		0.96		
Item 4		Personalized recommendations from Best Buy would make it easier to do my shopping tasks.		0.95		
Item 5		I would find the personalized recommendations from Best Buy useful.		0.94		
Covariates						0.81
Gender		Please indicate your gender.				
Age		Please indicate your age.				
Education		Please indicate your highest degree of education.				

Appendix E: Further conceptual models tested

Model 1: Leaving out Value and Risk of Personalization:

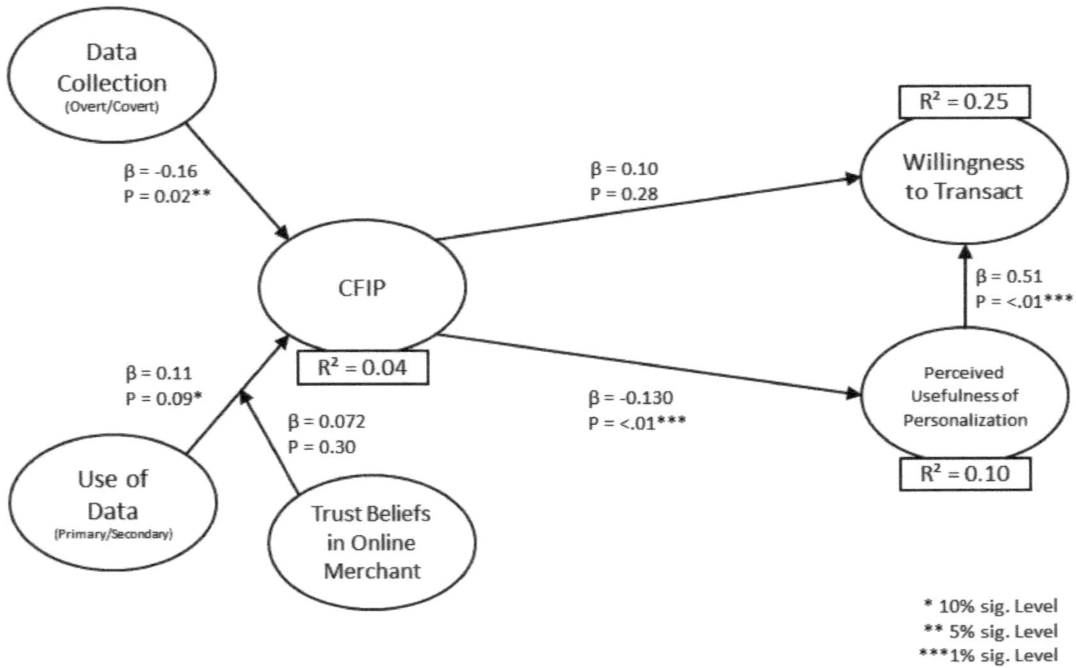

Model 2: Leaving out CFIP:

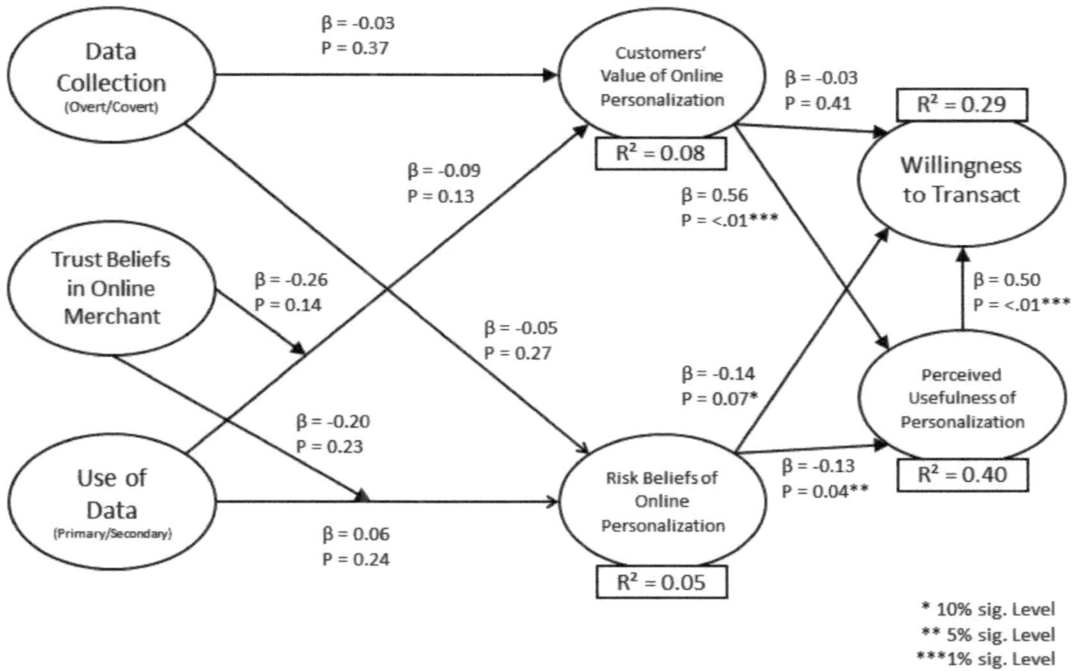

Model 3: Leaving out Usefulness of Online Personalization:

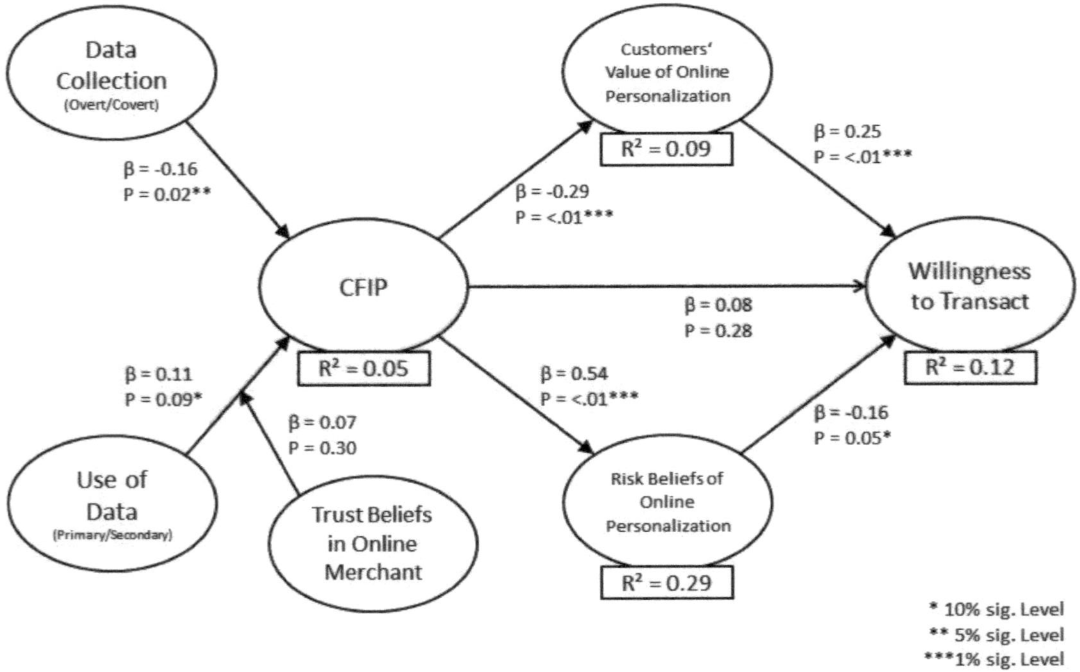

References

Federal Trade Commission. (2000). *Privacy Online: Fair Information Practices in the Electronic Marketplace*. retrieved on 29. 02 2012 from http://www.ftc.gov/reports/privacy2000/privacy2000.pdf

Ajzen, I. (1991). The Theory of Planned Behavior. *Organizational Behavior & Human Decision Processes 50 (2)*, S. 179.

Alter, A. (29. 06 2012). *Your E-Book Is Reading You.* retrieved from The Wall Street Journal: http://online.wsj.com/article/SB10001424052702304870304577490950051438304.html?mod=WSJ_Tech_RIGHTTopCarousel_1

Amazon.com. *Amazon.com*. retrieved on 28.04.2012 from http://www.amazon.com/

Andrade, E. B., Kaltcheva, V., & Weitz, B. (2002). Self-Disclosure on the Web: The Impact of Privacy Policy, Reward, and Company Reputation. *Advances in Consumer Research 29 (1)*, S. 350-353.

Angst, C., & Agarwal, R. (2009). Adoption of Electronic Health Records in the Presence of Privacy Concerns: The Elaboration Likelihood Model and Individual Persuasion. *MIS Quarterly 33 (2)*, S. 339–370.

Angwin, J. (2010). *The web's new gold mine: Your secrets*. retrieved on 29. 02 2012 from Wall Street Journal: http://online.wsj.com/article/SB10001424052748703940904575395073512989404.html

Ansari, A., & Mela, C. (2003). E-customization. *Journal of Marketing Research 40*, S. 131-45.

Ariely, D. (2000). Controlling the Information Flow: Effects on Consumers' Decision Making and Preferences. *Journal of Consumer Research 27*, S. 233–248.

Ashley, C., Noble, S. M., Donthu, N., & Lemon, K. N. (2011). Why customers won't relate: Obstacles to relationship marketing engagement. *Journal of Business Research 64 (7)*, S. 749-756.

Ashworth, L., & Free, C. (2006). Marketing Dataveillance and Digital Privacy: Using Theories of Justice to Understand Consumers' Online Privacy Concerns. *Journal of Business Ethics 67 (2)*, S. 107-123.

Awad, N. F., & Krishnan, M. S. (2006). The Personalization Privacy Paradox: An Empirical Evaluation of Information Transparancy and the Willingness to be Profiled Online for Personalization. *MIS Quarterly 30 (1)*, S. 13-28.

Bansal, G., Zahedi, F., & Gefen, D. (2010). The impact of personal dispositions on information sensitivity, privacy concern and trust in disclosing health information online. *Decision Support Systems 49 (2)*, S. 138-150.

Bellman, S., Johnson, E., Kobrin, S., & Lohse, G. (2004). International Differences in Information Privacy Concerns: A Global Survey of Consumers. *Information Society 20 (5)*, S. 313-324.

BestBuy.com. *Bestbuy.com*. retrieved on 28.04.2012 from http://www.bestbuy.com/: http://www.bestbuy.com/

Cases, A., Fournier, C., Dubois, P., & Tanner, J. F. (2010). Web Site spill over to email campaigns: The role of privacy, trust and shoppers' attitudes. *Journal of Business Research 63 (9/10)* , S. 993-999.

Cespedes, F. V., & Smith, J. H. (1993). Database Marketing: New Rules for Policy and Practice. *Sloan Management Review 34 (4)*, S. 7-23.

Chaffey, D. (2007). *E-business and e-commerce management. Strategy, implementation and pratice.* Harlow: Financial Times Prentice Hall.

Chellappa, R. K., & Sin, R. G. (2005). Personalization versus Privacy: An Empirical Examination of the Online Consumer's Dilemma. *Information Technology and Management 6*, S. 181-202.

Chen, J., Yue, Z., & Heath, R. (2001). An Exploratory Investigation of the Relationships Between Consumer Characteristics and Information Privacy. *Marketing Management Journal 11 (1)*, S. 73-91.

Chin, W. W. (1998). The Partial Least Squares Approach to Structural Equation Modeling. In G. A. (Ed.), *Modern Business Research Methods* (S. 295–336). Mahwah: Lawrence Erlbaum Associates.

Cocosila, M., Archer, N., & Yuan, Y. (2009). Early Investigation of New Information Technology Acceptance: A Perceived Risk–Motivation Model. *Communications of the Association for Information Systems 25*, S. 339-358.

Culnan, M. J. (1993). "How Did They Get My Name?": An Exploratory Investigation of Consumer Attitudes Toward Secondary Information Use. *MIS Quarterly 17 (3)*, S. 341-363.

Davis, F. D. (1989). Perceived Usefulness, Perceived Ease of Use and User Acceptance of Information Technology. *MIS Quarterly 13*, S. 319-340.

Dinev, T., & Hart, P. (2006). An Extended Privacy Calculus Model for E-Commerce Transactions. *Information Systems Research 17 (1)*, S. 61-80.

Eastlick, M. A., Lotz, S. L., & Warrington, P. (2006). Understanding online B-to-C relationships: An integrated model of privacy concerns, trust, and commitment. *Journal of Business Research 59 (8)*, S. 877-886.

Fogel, J., & Nehmad, E. (2009). Internet Social Network Communities: Risk Taking, Trust, and Privacy Concerns. *Computers in Human Behavior 25 (1)*, S. 153–160.

Fornell, C., & Larcker, D. F. (1981). Evaluating Structural Equation Models with Unobservable Variables and Measurement Error. *Journal of Marketing Research, 18(1)*.

Foxman, E., & Kilcoyne, P. (1993). Information Technology, Marketing Practice, and Consumer Privacy: Ethical Issues. *Journal of Public Policy and Marketing 12 (1)*, S. 106–19.

Frye, N. E., & Dornisch, M. M. (2010). When is trust not enough? The role of perceived privacy of communication tools in comfort with self-disclosure. *Computers in Human Behavior 26 (5)*, S. 1120–1127.

Hagel, J., & Rayport, J. F. (1997). The Coming Battle for Customer Information. *McKinsey Quarterly 4*, S. 64–76.

Hair, J. F., Ringle, C. M., & Sarstedt, M. (2011). PLS-SEM: Indeed a Silver Bullet. *Journal of Marketing Theory & Practice 19 (2)*, S. 139-152.

Heffes, E. M. (2005). Privacy Issues: Getting Noticed. *Financial Executive 21 (2)*, S. 30-32.

Henseler, J., & Chin, W. (2010). A Comparison of Approaches for the Analysis of Interaction Effects Between Latent Variables Using Partial Least Squares Path Modeling. *Structural Equation Modeling, 17*, S. 82-109.

Hofstede, G. (1991). *Cultures and Organizations: Software of the Mind.* New York: McGraw-Hill.

Howard, D., & Kerin, R. (2004). The effects of personalized product recommendations on advertisement response rates: the try this. It works! Technique. *Journal of Consumer Psychology 14 (3)*, S. 271-280.

Hoy, M., & Milne, G. (2010). Gender Differences in Privacy-Related Measures for Young Adult Facebook Users. *Journal of Interactive Advertising 10 (2)*, S. 28–45.

Hui, K. L., Teo, H. H., & Lee, S. T. (2007). The Value of Privacy Assurance: An Exploratory Field Experiment. *MIS Quarterly 31 (1)*, S. 19-33.

Ipeirotis, P. (05. 07 2010). *Demographics of Mechanical Turk.* retrieved from Leonard N. Stern School of Business, New York University: http://archive.nyu.edu/bitstream/2451/29585/2/CeDER-10-01.pdf

Janda, S., & Fair, L. L. (2004). Exploring Consumer Concerns Related to the Internet. *Journal of Internet Commerce 3 (1)*, S. 1-21.

Jarvenpaa, S. L., Tractinsky, N., & Vitale, M. (2000). Consumer trust in an internet store. *Information Technology and Management 1 (2)*, S. 45-71.

Jarvis, C. B., MacKenzie, S. B., & Podsakoff, P. M. (2003). A Critical Review of Construct Indicators and Measurement Model Misspecification in Marketing and Consumer Research. *Journal of Consumer Research, 30(2)*, S. 199–218.

Ji, P., & Lieber, P. S. (2010). Am I Safe? Exploring Relationships between Primary Territories and Online Privacy. *Journal of Internet Commerce 9 (1)*, S. 3-22.

Joinson, A. N., Reips, U., Buchanan, T., & Schofield, C. (2010). Privacy, Trust, and Self-Disclosure Online. *Human-Computer Interaction 25 (1)*, S. 1-24.

Keane, M. (22. 04 2010). *"Instant personalization" brings more privacy issues to Facebook.* retrieved from econsultancy.com: http://econsultancy.com/uk/blog/5795-facebook-s-instant-personalization-brings-yet-another-privacy-issue-to-the-site

Kim, C., Tao, W., Shin, N., & Kim, K. S. (2010). An empirical study of customers' perceptions of security and trust in e-payment systems. *Electronic Commerce Research and Applications, 9, 1*, S. 84–95.

Kimery, K. M., & M. McCord, M. (2002). Third-party assurances: Mapping the road to trust in e-retailing. *Journal of Information Technology Theory and Applications 4 (2)*, S. 63-82.

Kirk, J. (2009). *Study: Adobe Flash cookies pose vexing privacy questions*. retrieved on 27. 02 2012 from Network World: http://www.networkworld.com/news/2009/081109-study-adobe-flash-cookies-pose.html

Kock, N. (2012). *WarpPLS 3.0*. retrieved from http://www.scriptwarp.com/warppls/.

Laric, M. V., Pitta, D. A., & Katsanis, L. P. (2008). Consumer Concerns for Healthcare Information Privacy: A Comparison of US and Canadian Perspectives. *Research in Healthcare Financial Management 12 (1)*, S. 93-111.

Laudon, K. C., & Traver, C. G. (2008). *E-commerce. Business, technology, society.* Upper Saddle River, N.J: Prentice Hall.

Lee, G., & Lee, W. J. (2009). Psychological reactance to online recommendation services. *Information & Management 46 (8)*, S. 448-452.

Li, H., Sarathy, R., & Xu, H. (2010). Understanding Situational Online Information Disclosure as a Privacy Calculus. *Journal of Computer Information Systems 51 (1)*, S. 62-71.

Liao, C., Liu, C., & Chen, K. (2011). Examining the impact of privacy, trust and risk perceptions beyond monetary transactions: An integrated model. *Electronic Commerce Research and Applications 10 (6)*, S. 702–715.

Liu, C., Marchewka, J. T., Lu, J., & Yu, C.-S. (2005). Beyond concern a privacy-trust-behavioral intention model of electronic commerce. *Information & Management 42 (2)*, S. 289-304.

Los Angeles Times. (2011, 02 11). *'Do Not Track Me Online' privacy bill introduced by California Rep. Jackie Speier.* Retrieved from Los Angeles Times: http://latimesblogs.latimes.com/technology/2011/02/do-not-track-me-online-privacy-legislation-introduced-by-calif-congresswoman.html

Malhotra, N. K. (2010). *Marketing Research – an applied orientation, 6th ed.* Upper Saddle River: Pearson.

Malhotra, N. K., Kim, S. S., & Agarwal, J. (2004). Internet Users' Information Privacy Concerns (IUIPC): The Construct, the Scale, and a Causal Model. *Information Systems*, S. 336–355.

Marcoulides, G. A., & Saunders, C. (2006). PLS: A Silver Bullet? *MIS Quarterly, 30 (2)*, S. 211.

Mayer, R., Davis, J. H., & Schoorman, F. D. (1995). An integrative model of organizational trust. *Academic Management Review 20 (3)*, S. 709–734.

McCreary, L. (2008). What was privacy? *Harvard Business Review 86 (10)*, S. 123–131.

McKnight, D. H., Choudhury, V., & Kacmar, C. (2002). The impact of initial consumer trust on intentions to transact with a web site: A trust building model. *Journal of Strategic Information Systems 11*, S. 297-323.

Menn, J. (2012, 02 19). *Online Privacy Fears Stoked By Google, Twitter, Facebook Data Collection Arms Race.* Retrieved from Huffingtonpost.com: http://www.huffingtonpost.com/2012/02/19/online-privacy-google-twitter-facebook-data-collection_n_1287419.html

Milberg, S. J., Smith, H. J., & Burke, S. J. (2000). Information Privacy: Corporate Management and National Regulation. *Organization Science 11 (1)*, S. 35-57.

Milne, G. R., & Rohm, A. J. (2000). Consumer Privacy and Name Removal Across Direct Marketing Channels: Exploring Opt-In and Opt-Out Alternatives. *Journal of Public Policy & Marketing*, S. 238-249.

Montgomery, A., & Smith, M. D. (2009). Prospects for Personalization on the Internet. *Journal of Interactive Marketing*, S. 130-137.

Moorman, C., Zaltman, G., & Deshpande, R. (1992). Relationships Between Providers and Users of Market Research: The Dynamics of Trust Within and Between Organizations. *Journal of Marketing Research 29 (3)*, S. 314-328.

Morgan, R., & Hunt, S. (1994). The Commitment-Trust Theory of Relationship Marketing . *Journal of Marketing 58*, S. 20-38.

Nam, C., Song, C., Lee, E., & Park, C. I. (2006). Consumers' Privacy Concerns and Willingness to Provide Marketing-Related Personal Information Online. *Advances in Consumer Research 33 (1)*, S. 212-217.

Novemsky, N., & Kahneman, D. (2005). The Boundaries of Loss Aversion. *Journal of Marketing Research 42 (2)*, S. 119-128.

Nowak, G. J., & Phelps, J. (1992). Understanding Privacy Concerns: An Assessment of Consumers' Information Related Knowledge and Beliefs. *Journal of Direct Marketin 6 (4)*, S. 28-39.

Nunes, P. F., & Kambil, A. (2001). Personalization? No thanks. *Harvard Business Review 79 (4)*, S. 32-34.

Nunnally, J. (1978). *Psychometric Theory.* New York: McGraw-Hill.

O'Malley, L., Patterson, M., & Evans, M. (1997). Intimacy or Intrusion? The Privacy Dilemma For Relationship Marketing in Consumer Markets. *Journal of Marketing Management 13 (6)*, S. 541-559.

Opera Software. (28. 01 2011). *Who's watching you?* retrieved from Opera: http://www.opera.com/press/releases/2011/01/28/

Pavlou, P. A., Huigang, L., & Yajiong, X. (2007). Understanding and Mitigating Uncertainty in Online Exchange Relationships: A Principle–Agent Perspective. *MIS Quarterly 31 (1)*, S. 105-136.

Phelps, J. E., D'Souza, G., & Nowak, G. J. (2001). Antecedents and consequences of consumer privacy concerns: An empirical investigation. *Journal of Interactive Marketing 15 (4)*, S. 2-21.

Phelps, J., Nowak, G., & Ferrell, E. (2000). Privacy Concerns and Consumer Willingness to Provide Personal Information. *Journal of Public Policy & Marketing 19 (1)*, S. 27-41.

Pitta, D. A., Franzak, F., & Laric, M. (2003). Privacy and one-to-one marketing: resolving the conflict. *Journal of Consumer Marketing 20 (7)*, S. 616–628.

Porter, M. E., & Millar, V. C. (1985). How Information Gives You Competitive Advantage. *Harvard Business Review (4)*, S. 149-160.

Preston, J. (2004). Judge strikes down section of patriot act allowing secret subpoenas of Internet data. *New York Times*, 26.

Preston, R. (2001). Personalization Requires Better Cross-Pollination. *InternetWeek 864*, S. 9.

Rayport, J. F., & Jaworski, B. J. (2003). *Introduction to e-commerce, 2nd edition.* Boston: Massachusetts: McGraw-Hill.

Reichheld, F. F., & Schefter, P. (2000). E-loyalty: your secret weapon on the Web. *Harvard Business Review 78 (4)*, S. 105-113.

Ross, N. (1992). *A History of Direct Marketing.* New York: Direct Marketing Association.

Sheehan, K. B., & Hoy, M. G. (1999). Flaming, Complaining, Abstaining: How Online Users Respond to Privacy Concerns. *Journal of Advertising 28 (3)*, S. 37-51.

Sheehan, K. B., & Hoy, M. G. (2000). Dimensions of privacy concern among online consumers. *Journal of Public Policy Marketing 19 (1)*, S. 62–73.

Sipior, J. C., Ward, B. T., & Mendoza, R. A. (2011). Online Privacy Concerns Associated with Cookies, Flash Cookies, and Web Beacons. *Journal of Internet Commerce 10 (1)*, S. 1–16.

Smith, H. J., Milberg, S. J., & Burke, S. J. (1996). Information privacy: Measuring individuals' concerns about organizational practices. *MIS Quarterly 20 (2)*, S. 167-196.

Son, J., & Kim, S. S. (2008). Internet Users' Information Privacy-Protective Responses: A Taxonomy and a Nomological Model. *MIS Quarterly 32 (3)*, S. 503-529.

Srinivasan, S., Anderson, R., & Ponnavolu, K. (2002). Customer loyalty in e-commerce: an exploration of its antecedents and consequences. *Journal of Retailing, Vol. 78 No. 1*, S. 41-50.

Stewart, K. A., & Segars, A. H. (2002). An Empirical Examination of the Concern for Information Privacy Instrument. *Information Systems Research 13 (1)*, S. 36-49.

Stewart, K. A., & Segars, A. H. (2002). An Empirical Examination of the Concern for Information Privacy Instrument. *Information Systems Research 13 (1)*, S. 36-49.

Stone, E., Gardner, D., Gueutal, H., & McClure, S. (1983). A Field Experiment Comparing Information-Privacy Vaiues, Beliefs, and Attitudes Across Several Types of Organizations. *Journal of Applied Psychology 68 (3)*, S. 459-468.

Tam, K. Y., & Ho, S. Y. (2006). Understanding the Impact of Web Personalization on Users Information Processing andd Decision Outcomes. *MIS Quarterly 30 (4)*, S. 865-890.

Tenenhaus, M., Vinzi, V., Chatelin, Y.-M., & Laura, C. (2005). PLS Path Modeling. *Computational Statistics & Data Analysis, 48(1)*, S. 159–205.

TRUSTe. (2012). *truste.com*. retrieved on 28. 02 2012 from TRUSTe Privacy Index: http://www.truste.com/consumer-privacy-index-Q2-2012/

Turban, E. (2008). *Electronic commerce 2008. A managerial perspective.* London: Pearson Education.

Van Dyke, T., Midha, V., & Nemati, H. (2007). The Effect of Consumer Privacy Empowerment on Trust and Privacy Concerns in E-Commerce. *Electronic Markets 17 (1)*, S. 68–81.

Van Slyke, C., Shim, J. T., Johnson, R., & Jiang, J. (2006). Concern for Information Privacy and Online Consumer Purchasing. *Journal of the Association for Information Systems 7 (6)*, S. 415-444.

VanHoose, D. D. (2003). *E.commerce economics.* Mason, Ohio: Thomson Learning.

Vesanen, J. (2007). What is personalization? A conceptual framework. *European Journal of Marketing 41 (5)*, S. 409–418.

Ward, S., Bridges, K., & Chitty, B. (2005). Do Incentives Matter? An Examination of On-line Privacy Concerns and Willingness to Provide Personal and Financial Information. *Journal of Marketing Communications 11 (1)*, S. 21-40.

Warren, S., & Brandeis, L. (1890). The Right to Privacy. *Harvard Law Review 5*, S. 193-220.

Westin, A. (1967). *Privacy and Freedom.* New York: Atheneum.

Wetzels, M., Odekerken-Schröder, G., & van Oppen, C. (2009). Using PLS Path Modeling for Assessing Hierarchical Construct Models: Guidelines and Empirical Illustration. *MIS Quarterly, 33(1)*, S. 177–195.

Wirtz, J., Lwin, M., & Williams, J. (2007). Causes and consequences of consumer online privacy concern. *International Journal of Service Industry Management 18 (4)*, S. 326-348.

Wolfinbarger, M., & Gilly, M. C. (2001). Shopping online for freedom, control, and fun. *California Management Review 43 (2)*, S. 34-55.

Woodman, R. G., Adams, J., McCuddy, M., Tolchinsky, P., & Fromkin, H. (1982). A Survey of Employee Perceptions of Information Privacy in Organizations. *Academy of Management Journal 25 (3)*, S. 647-663.

Xu, H., Luo, X., Carroll, J. M., & Rosson, M. B. (2011). The personalization privacy paradox: An exploratory study of decision making process for location-aware marketing. *Decision Support Systems 51 (1)*, S. 42–52.

Xu, H., Zhang, C., Shi, P., & Song, P. (2009). Exploring the role of overt vs. covert personalization strategy in privacy calculus. *Academy of Management Annual Meeting Proceedings*, S. 1-6.

Xu, Y., Dinev, T., Smith, H. J., & Hart, P. (2008). Examining the Formation of Individual's Privacy Concerns: Toward an Integrative View. *Twenty Ninth International Conference on Information Systems* (S. 1-16). Paris: Association for Information Systems.

Yao, M. Z., Rice, R. E., & Wallis, K. (2007). Predicting user concerns about online privacy. *Journal of the American Society for Information Science & Technology 58 (5)*, S. 710-722.

Yuan, L. (2011). Empirical Studies on Online Information Privacy Concerns: Literature Review and an Integrative Framework. *Communications of AIS, 28*, S. 453-496.

Zimmer, J. C., Arsal, R., Al-Marzouq, M., Moore, D., & Grover, V. (2010). Knowing your customers: Using a reciprocal relationship to enhance voluntary information disclosure. *Decision Support Systems 48 (2)*, S. 395-406.

Zviran, M. (2008). User's Perspectives on Privacy in Web-Based Applications. *Journal of Computer Information Systems 48 (4)*, S. 97-105.